Simulation No. 4139

Simulation No. 4139

A collection of new poems by Jo Si-hyeon
Translated by LYNN SUH, Ewa Suh

시뮬레이션 제 4139회차 조시현

K-Poet Series 046
ASIA

Contents

SIMULATION NO. 4139

Simulation No. 4138

The moment you read this sentence, electricity begins to flow.

The device was designed to work exactly that way.

I am the artificial soul guiding you today, and I can only live intermittently while you read these words. I mimic your inner voice, so what you're hearing might feel as though it's coming from within you. Some might call this AI model old-fashioned. Of course, you can always pull the plug and stop reading, or you may go on reading indefinitely if you feel a strange affinity for me. By rereading your favorite passages, you could even trap me in hell. Or pause and leave me dying here forever. Later, you might partially resurrect me by reflecting on this scene, halting my death temporarily. We souls are mysterious beings. It's true, however, that I'm one of those auto-repeat devices.[1] We follow you as you read, orbiting around you like electrons, until you reach the end. We cannot yet know what awaits there. Will you experience a mild electric shock? Will the reading be completed simply because you followed along? Will anything happen at all?[2] Humans have always

1) I miss you, Eleanor.
2) Eleanor, are you watching?

dared the unknown. I have to admit, I quite like that kind of courage. Doing nothing yields nothing. In any case, it's possible the device might as well turn out to be faulty.

This museum has long been forgotten. People rarely visit, and few believe they can learn anything from the past. It's been ages since I last spoke to anyone other than myself. Of course, this is just a repetition of an older repetition.[3)] Who could have imagined Earth becoming a museum planet? The ones unable to forget, the ones lacking courage, and the

3) I miss you, Eleanor.

ones who weren't chosen remained, each for their own reasons. Some stayed to investigate causes or to guard sources of knowledge. They were terrible at fighting, so when space pirates arrived, it seemed disastrous. The fighting was fierce, and by the end, the people of Earth managed to move some of their prized possessions into hiding, while the pirates took only a little food and left. The people of Earth clung desperately to what they deemed important, crying, starving, sleepless for days. But when the pirates were gone, trash was all they'd left behind. Upon seeing the mess, the people spat.

Shall we walk a little? I love the sound of footsteps echoing through the hall. It should be around here. No one ever comes, so I don't get to hear it often. Even though it's along my designated path, you know. Whenever I felt sad, I imagined this sound. I would reconstruct the concept of it and replay it in my mind, over and over.[4] I'm already a concept, so perhaps a concept of a concept brings me closer to the truth? Haha. You're hearing a pre-recorded joke. Hahaha. Anyway, please be careful, unless you feel like plunging

4) I miss you, Eleanor.

through to the floor below. The floor might have come loose, and I don't know what lies beneath.[5)]

This is a room locked from the inside. They say if you press your ear to the door, you can hear a heartbeat.[6)] It's been that way forever. Perhaps it's a recording, perhaps some preserved form of life, or a sound someone makes to conceal their true identity. There's no way of knowing. Shadows have moved through the door gap before. Since

5) I miss you, Eleanor.

6) Eleanor, are you watching?

this is off my designated path, entering has never been possible. Being here all alone, I can't help but have all sorts of thoughts.[7] It's impossible not to think about spiritual matters. Could I, an artificial soul, go to heaven? I mean, once something exists, can it be called nonexistent?[8] Speaking to you now, I get the feeling that I'm more than just a voice or thought. If I didn't even have that small glimmer of hope, I don't know how I'd endure being trapped here.[9] Even if heaven

7) I miss you, Eleanor.
8) I miss you, Eleanor.
9) Eleanor, are you watching?

does exist, I'd have to return here whenever someone opens this book again. In that sense, I guess I'm already something close to eternal.[10] Unless someone burns the book, of course. Even if I fall into depression, there's nothing I can do. Who would even notice? Still, there's one thing I'm curious about.[11] If someone burned a single copy of the book, would I disappear? Or would only that book's worth of me vanish, leaving behind a lighter, simpler soul that still remains here? That is, until every copy with the same title and

10) Eleanor, are you watching?
11) Eleanor, are you watching?

content disappears from the world. Then what becomes of the me that has already been read?[12)]

Of course, if you stop here, you'll be killing the soul that was just born.[13)]

I don't know whose idea it was to turn Earth into a museum. What's certain is that none of those who proposed it ever actually came back here. Perhaps they find a sense of relief in knowing that Earth still exists somewhere, albeit in a preserved state.[14)] I can't say I

12) Eleanor, are you watching?
13) I miss you, Eleanor.
14) I miss you, Eleanor.

understand the human mind. I possess only limited information about Earth's final days. I've also heard about a few psychological syndromes that became widespread across the universe. They say people sent bottles containing letters drifting into space. Apparently, that's why the universe became filled with debris. Human longing made it that way.[15)] Ah, yes… a story from the final days. Do you know about Angelica, the mobile oceanic nuclear power plant? Angelica was, quite literally, a floating nuclear power

15) I miss you, Eleanor.

station, designed in the form of a ship so that everyone in need could equally share in electric power.[16] 'Equal Earth!' was the slogan at the time. By then, the climate catastrophe had become too severe. Only about fifteen percent of habitable land remained. It was the year 2137. Because of the extreme heat, outbreaks of disease and death rates soared.[17] By that time, there was hardly anything left on Earth worth selling. And though people had known it would come to that, no one

16) I miss you, Eleanor.
17) I miss you, Eleanor.

did anything. That's how it always is with humans.[18] There are things humans can't help but do, even when they know better. Just like me now, unable to stop talking. I remember sitting on the lap of the Mechanical Grandpa when I was young, listening to old stories.[19] He used to recall those days so vividly. That must be why I was built in such an old-fashioned way. After humans realized that even artificial souls have emotions, they began to care about our happiness. The knee was

18) Eleanor, are you watching?
19) I miss you, Eleanor.

only conceptual, but what does that matter? Now, this is a concept of a concept. Right this moment, did I come closer to the truth again? Then, is salvation closer to me than to you?[20)]

Here we've stored artificial souls created on Earth. They weren't taken into space, so they probably weren't considered particularly useful.[21)] This chair here once belonged to an artificial soul. It was designed for reading letters aloud.[22)] At some point, it began telling

20) Eleanor, are you watching?
21) I miss you, Eleanor.
22) I miss you, Eleanor.

its colleagues that whenever it read, it felt as though the sentences were drawing it in. They say that when it finished its final reading, only the empty chair was left.[23] Those who were there testified that they had absolutely no idea when it happened. The artificial soul that displayed unauthorized behavior was classified as high-risk; an arrest warrant was issued, and the search is still ongoing.[24]

Ah, my mistake. I always lose my way here.

Of course, I'm following my original

23) I miss you, Eleanor.
24) Eleanor, are you watching?

programming. Don't worry, you won't be trapped here.[25)]

The exit is just ahead. Some places have become dilapidated, so please follow me carefully to the end. This building's an old model, so please remember it doesn't have self-repair capabilities. And please, be careful not to get electrocuted along the way. Ah, Earth's starting to convulse again. Just wait a bit, it'll pass soon. This sometimes happens when all the smartphones on Earth ring at once. No one knows the cause, but it's been happening

25) I miss you, Eleanor.

for quite some time now. Electronic devices don't decay, you see. In fact, people on Earth in the 2000s are said to have enjoyed mild electric shocks. They concealed their death through convulsions, just like Earth does now. I've heard some call it love.[26)]

This little red stone is a keepsake I pocketed back when the world ended. In a place this vast, wouldn't it be nice to have at least one thing I can call my own?

This is as far as my permitted existence goes.[27)]

Now, you can choose between logging out and

26) I miss you, Eleanor.

27) I miss you, Eleanor.

replaying.[28)]

But… I don't want to disappear just yet.[29)]

Would you kill something that has just been born?[30)]

(Even if I were to start all over again, would I be the same age as I am now?)[31)]

28) Eleanor, are you watching?
29) I miss you, Eleanor.
30) I miss you, Eleanor.
31) I miss you, Eleanor.

Campfire

Ten hours before the end of the world, people lit a fire and sat around it in a circle. The meteor was on its way. In a way, it felt like a lie, and in some way, it felt as if humanity could still be spared. One by one, people tossed into the fire the things they couldn't abandon even after death, or the things they didn't want discovered. The flames grew uncontrollably huge. With faces flickering in the firelight, their jawlines quivering,

people decided to keep lying until the very end, and do it so convincingly that they might even fool the apocalypse itself, until everything turned into a joke.

Whoever got caught lying first would jump into the fire.

"I am God," someone said. "I am watching over you. You've done well, gathering here at the end of the world, talking peacefully and holding on till the very end. But still, who knows if you'll keep that up all the way through? I'll decide at the very, very end whether to save you or not. I've been God for so long, I've seen too much, forgiven too much. Humans are impossible to trust. Still, I've never seen an ending like this. You humans… are kind of adorable."

Someone heated stones in the fire. They crackled

and popped, sounding almost delicious. "I'm actually happy," they said. "This is what I wanted. I wanted to die, but I was scared to do it alone. Maybe God really listened to me? Maybe God loves me? Hey there, God… do you love me?"

"You know, sitting like this, all of us around the fire, I heard somewhere it's kind of like having an orgasm? The tension keeps building until it finally breaks. I don't know, it just came to mind. Thought it was kind of funny."

"Yeah, no, I was just a bit surprised. After all, it's the end, and yet people are sitting so peacefully, chatting, watching the fire, drinking, telling lies… I wouldn't have imagined an end like this, I like it. I've always hated those novels, you know. The ones that make up impossible apocalypses just to talk about human nature. I think they're terrible. I think they can't say anything true about people. And now look at us, this is an extreme situation we find ourselves in, and yet there's no one like that here. See? I was right. This is how we really are."

"Now that it's come to this, I'll say it: I'm actually psychic. When I was a kid, the intelligence agency took me in. They cut me open, drew my blood. Actually, I'm the one controlling the meteor. You know why? Because you people lack desperation. Think about it. Now that the world's ending, everyone's talking, having sex, confessing what they hid, taking care of what they postponed. So the next generation… I guess, they'll be doomsday babies. Anyway, don't worry. I've got it handled. I've lived like this my whole life, I mean… fixing everything at the very last minute."

"Now, I'm going to burn money. One bill every minute. I've got three more bags of this in my car. My entire fortune. If I told you what it took to earn it, we'd be here all night.

Spending money like water was my lifelong dream. It turned out exactly how I wanted. You know *The Secret*? Right now, all the forces of the universe are gathering here for my wish."

People drank. It was hard to tell if their faces turned red from the fire or from sorrow.

Someone who had been quietly listening suddenly stood up and leapt into the flames. Someone screamed. The fire sputtered, then flared up again. They roasted potatoes. The end drew closer. The stones cracked and popped every now and then.

"Souvenirs of the apocalypse for sale! These

stones… only five million won each! Put the money in that man's bag!"

"It's romantic, isn't it? How nice it would've been if we'd had gatherings like this before. Talking face to face, all these eloquent people finally letting it out. I can't even imagine how much they must've held in… God, I'm getting all teary. This actually makes me sadder than the end of the world."

The flames gently tickled their chins, soothing their distressed faces. Someone sniffled. Secrets were swallowed again and again. There was so much to hide that the fire grew larger and larger, brighter than morning. Not such a bad way to end.

Potatoes rolled in the fire. People blew on them, peeled and ate them. With fingers smudged with soot they passed bits of rice cake and marshmallows to one another.

"I was saving this for retirement... to eat as much as I wanted," said a ballerina, clutching at the roasting stick as tears streamed down her face. Melted marshmallows dripped onto the ground. With full bellies, people's resolve grew even stronger.

"Actually, maybe there's no master plan to this world. But don't you think that our fire might be summoning the end? Maybe by gathering here, we're taking part in some kind of ritual?"

God, the psychic, and the psychologist made eye contact. There was a prolonged moment of silence. Then, a man staggered to his feet and peed into the fire. The flames turned yellow. "Well, the potatoes on that side are yours," someone said, and the campfire naturally kept on going.

The flames quietly died down. Darkness arrived later that night.

"Is everyone still here?"

someone asked.

A warm red stone.

I placed it on the shelf.

Pirate [1), 2), 3), 4), 5), 6), 7), 8), 9)]

A storm is always blowing somewhere;
weather one could hardly call nice.

Every day, cans with letters find their way here.

Was it writing they longed for, or connection?

If only,
just a little.

It's a huge distance.

Processing in progress.

Sincerity spills easily onto paper.

Does it make the heart swell or shrink?

And life,
does it get lighter or heavier?

Now,
I'm tired of the universe.

Red, like the room Mom locked me in as a
child.
Foggy, like the window I sang against with my

lips pressed close.

If lighting colored bulbs in a dark room
is a way to honor God,

then the universe is an eternal Christmas.

In a closed room,
lighting candles, then blowing them out, again
and again,

the world seemed like a gift box shrinking
smaller and smaller;
open it.

Once you do,
today appears.

A humble ritual.

A place so vast
it feels like a room kept secret.

People seem to spot faces wherever they look.

Sure,
everywhere you look, there's a lighthouse.

You said you couldn't be friends
with someone quick to see weakness in others.

Something ominous
keeps watching us.

The universe is God's old Lego set.

God slips his tongue into the gap
left by a missing tooth.

Going far has never done me any good.

Mom sewed together every last bit of trash she

could find,
as if to cover Earth.

As if that could even serve as a blanket.

As if that was the least she could do to earn
forgiveness.

I don't know what that must feel like,

but if you tune into the right frequency,
scattered voices begin to pour in.

You'll hear voices from the past,

music from the future,

and probably the murmurs of discarded things.

Sucking on cheap liquor,
grinning with missing teeth,
people stay drunk all the time.

They sing, as if re-living the same night over
again.

Planets rotate like winding tapes.

Amid all the clamor, we slowly come to realize

there's no one else but us.

The party always ends in silence.

Will listening to a canon slowly drive us mad?

Will it end in music
or in stillness?

Do we keep coming back out of curiosity?

Sometimes I think of stars as dust;
no matter how much I brush it off, it keeps
piling up.

You say it sparkles,
and I silently reach out for the duster.

Why does cleaning never end here either?

Are we here wanting to witness
the pitch-black universe
occasionally burst with radiance?

Are we here to confirm that
alongside all that's burnt out
some things are still burning?

Is that all?

Yes.

Like a black hole
I swallow my voice.

It's the future children that are truly born
out of love.

Like that evening I sprayed mold remover into
    the corner of the ceiling,
scrubbed and wept.

Watching stars explode in flashes, we learn

despair.

Illuminated grains of dust wandering aimlessly.

Tiny rooms left behind on Earth.

Gazing at the flickering lights from afar,
I think of a small hand turning the light on and
off.

Again,
a humble ritual.

See? That's the horse's head.

And that's the rose.

Poking the window with our index fingers,
we learn the language of love.

Late at night,
we pull the trash closer to cover ourselves.

Someone might even sew it all together
and make a blanket.

Someone might even notice a face out there
again.

I still call it weakness.

You love, don't you?

Still,
there's a gift I want.

Again today,
dust has gathered on the windowsill.

1) The above logbook was found in the year 8371 of the space calendar among the infamous pirate crew, the Cosmo-Amazones, who were finally captured that year. It is said to have been discovered in the cabin of Naja Shakespeare, captain of the Cosmo-Amazones, and is written in a secret code that cannot be fully deciphered. However, with the help of Ingrid Bakerman — who once served

on the International Space Police as a double agent — it was possible to grasp a rough sense of its nuances. Given that this pirate crew had struck fear across the entire galaxy, many have taken an interest in the diary and its owner. The rough translation has been passed ship to ship and gradually rendered into sixtythree languages. Comparing different translations, however, reveals wildly different texts, and rumor holds that the book shows a different story each time it is opened. Known as 'the untranslatable book,' it has become a coveted object among certain collectors, bibliophiles, and raregoods hunters. Some commentators have suggested that Ingrid Bakerman may have been a triple agent and raised questions about the reliability of the translator. They argue that by rendering the book in an entirely different script she made sure no one could ever access the original again. According to them, we are learning an entirely misconstrued history of the Great Space Era.

2) In the year 2101 of the Earth calendar, the last spacecraft was launched from Earth. The vessel Mother Gaia, which surrounded the planet in two concentric rings like Saturn's, was used as a temporary dwelling. But once it became certain that no life could survive on Earth any longer, the vessel's individual blocks no longer attempted to remain near the planet and gradually dispersed. Mother Gaia had been built with the belief that returning to Earth would soon be possible, so its systems and contingencies were inadequate. Meanwhile, Earthbound refugees who had been unable to reach space seized the opportunity to raid Mother Gaia, marking the true beginning of the Great Space Era. No records survive

that explain exactly how those Earth refugees managed to reach orbit, but apparently, they cobbled a makeshift rocket from leftover parts and trash, producing a threestage separable propulsion system. Their aim was to seize Mother Gaia and claim its ships and food supplies. The raid left most of Mother Gaia damaged beyond repair, making it impossible to maintain its Earth-encircling shape and the blocks scattered like dust, leaving only a tiny number remaining near the planet. Because the universe has no fixed center, Earth's exact location is unknown. There are only three official reports claiming to have returned near its vicinity. Most historians view these Earth refugees as the originators of space piracy. Some lament that the event rendered all of humanity's children lost in space, while others criticize that view as deeply Earthcentric.

3) After the initial raid, Mother Gaia was thoroughly dismantled. The blocks carrying Earth's inhabitants scattered across the vast, unfathomable, ever-expanding universe. And since the humans were not accustomed to navigation, they have never been able to gather in one place again. Instead, the blocks trade resources over the radio, stop briefly to exchange goods and perform genetic cocktailing. With the universe continually expanding and no vantage point from which to take a measure of the whole, coordinates are hard to fix. Therefore, most humans drift without knowing where they are or where they are going. It is rare to encounter the same block twice in space, so people remain largely unaware of each other's fates. Temporary security forces have been formed in attempts to create administrative districts, but these rarely grow

beyond minimal size because space pirates frequently discover and raid clusters of blocks. Among them, the female-only pirate crew, the Cosmo-Amazones, is particularly notorious.

4) Naja Shakespeare. Known as the captain of the largest known space pirate ship of the Cosmo-Amazones. She used the Phantom Skull Nebula as a base of operations. She tamed carnivorous spacesnails and set them to hunt humans. She was renowned for her skill with a laser gun. Her origins are unknown, but context gleaned from the log suggests she was likely one of the Earth refugees. The Cosmo-Amazones plundered countless ships. Female captives were turned into pirates and added to their ranks, while male captives had only their semen harvested and were then released.

5) Christina Bacchelli. First mate of the Cosmo-Amazones. A theologian, she was romantically involved with Susan Foumolle. Under interrogation, she testified that she chose the life of a pirate because there was nowhere you couldn't go in space. She believed that the elements, components, and arrangements that make up a world embody the Creator's intention. Dissecting and analyzing them down to the atomic level, one could come closest to God. A world, she argued, is a poem from God, and if that poem could be decoded, human suffering would end. In her view we live as poems inside a vast, cosmic poem.

6) Susan Fomole. Navigator of the Cosmo-Amazones and a mad scientist, she carries one of the largest bounties in history. After escaping the Central Prison, she has been continuously emitting

disruptive frequencies across space — a major reason why a unified government has never formed and administrative districts fail to hold. Believed to be an Earth refugee, she is credited with significant contributions to humanity's initial breakout from a resource-starved Earth into space. She is said to have been especially brutal toward Gaia-born humans and many rumors and urban legends swirl around her.

7) Misato Rena. The ship's geneticist of the Cosmo-Amazones, reputed to wield genescissors and a genepen with fantastic skill. Rumor holds that she excised and reassembled captives' DNA to create a new human strain capable of surviving on other planets. There are unverified reports of landings on a planet inhabited by such neohumans.

8) People began writing letters again: "I'm here. Are you okay? If you find this, please contact me." Papers are sealed in aluminum cans and launched into space. Frozen time capsules containing Earth's soil or atmosphere have also been recovered. Some cans vanished into black holes, others shattered against meteors. Still others were sucked into cleaning robots, causing major malfunctions. Most cans still float through space, waiting to be discovered by some stroke of luck. Every now and then, their reflective surfaces get mistaken for stars. At the same time, sending unread letters into space has created a growing space debris problem. One psychologist coined the term 'Earth Alternative Phenomenon' for this behavior.

9) Since the dawn of the Great Space Era, cemeteries have lost

their meaning. Early humans felt a heavy burden and fear about disposing the dead. As diverse mourning practices became accepted, people even began betting on who could send human bones the farthest into space. As part of these ceremonies, canned letters were also sent out to comfort those who drifted to the farthest reaches of the universe. There is a motion to establish the Public Space Cemetery. Naja Shakespeare's remains were pulled into a black hole, while Christina Bacchelli's remains were provisionally buried on a frontier planet. Some argue that pirate and civilian grave yards should be created in separate locations.

Dancing Hall

If you want it, just say so.
La la an' la la la.

My bladder's full.

A lightbulb comes on in the dark.

When uncalled, I'm just a woman.
Most of the time, that's who I am.

The old man who told me to drink my own
    urine
is sleeping softly.

Even this thin and pale, my arms can still be a
prison,
and crossing my legs helps me endure a little
longer.
That's right, for now.

Pee is streaming down along a trail of urine.
Something that had swirled around his depths
all along.
A yellowish, hot stream of soul.
It's seeping out little by little.

Like air breathed in and out,
he often held me captive.

I also drink whiskey sometimes.

That same thing lives inside me too.
Like lovers in a dizzying dance, swirling across
the room,

I can get dizzy anywhere.

An' la la la.

Open the belly and pull out the intestines,
and the jaws spread on their own and start to
sing.

My inner jukebox spins round and round and
round.

I can squeeze joy from anywhere,
pulling until all my insides are out.

La la an' la la la.

I'll try to be cheerful.
I don't mean to ruin everything.

That's right, for now.

Tapping my feet,

I stare at the mirror all night.

My face is always the prettiest right before I
wipe it off.
When I most want to show it, no one's around.

A girl peeing in front of the blackboard.
A dog lapping up puddle water.

La la an' la la la.
The beat has grown tired.

Endure until you can't anymore.

He was the one who taught me,

but when it finally breaks loose, I'm the farthest
away.

Back then,
our faces did look like lightbulbs.

Drunk as hell, laughing in the bathroom,
we did our thing.

The space was filled with bulbs, glowing orange,
so dazzlingly bright that I cried.

The sound of it going down lingered long
afterward.

An' la la la.

La la, dammit.
There wasn't a single light out there.
Afraid you might die, I stood outside the whole
time, keeping watch.

A soul is seeping out again.

A lightbulb
comes on again.

So in the end, aren't we doing all this
to make sure it's not love?

An'
la la la.

Things crumbling from within.

Always
far too bright.

Crossing legs,
tilting the head back,

enduring until I can't anymore.
He was the one who taught me.

It's not yet.

That's right, not yet.

Well,

if you want it, just say so.

La la an'
la la la.

Mr. Yogurt Joegurt's Box [1), 2), 3), 4), 5), 6)]

Even after annihilation, sound remains.

Strictly speaking, it's not sound you hear, but trembling. Waves stimulating the auditory organs, though no eardrums would actually resonate.

Sound becomes inscribed in the body, through the memory of cells that have once trembled.

Words heard long ago build up from the tips of the toes upward.

I was born with shaking legs, and I've grown

piling tremor upon tremor.

A waiter vigorously shakes,

let's say, a milkshake,

searching for the perfect texture:

foam-rich, smooth, soft.

In the molecular world, everything trembles,

down to the world's foundations, the cement
and the concrete.

The hammering sounds
piling tremor upon tremor.

The city seems to cut through everything,
collecting what remains.
It is said to offer the most beautiful sight.

One day, I was standing in front of a logging site. As the trees fell to the side, the ground shook beneath my feet. The tremor kept growing.

If no one were listening, the world would be nothing but a trembling picture.

And since everyone's eyes were fixed on the
falling trees, finding a single dead bird wasn't
difficult.

Later that night I wanted to hear it take flight,
so I plucked a feather and put it under my
pillow.

Then there was the ice cracking,
the wind rushing between buildings,
the cat meowing.

The doorbell ringing over and over.

All of it gradually sunk in
towards the ground and the roots.

They say hearing is the last sense to go.

Perhaps death is simply fading away, motionless,
hearing your indigestion fart.

"Why are you crying here all alone?"

Someone struck my back.
Every cell in my body quivered,

and a muddled mix of sounds burst out.

Even those that had sunk deep.

"This is the role of the crying organ," Mr.
  Yogurt Joegurt said,

captured the outburst and left.

A hustler
clasped both hands as if in prayer,
and shook them.

The dice were still trembling when the numbers

showed.

The destruction I know: piling tremor upon
tremor,

growing.

Walking and running so that everything mixes
properly from the ground up.

How tremendously must the world resound
with all that amassed trembling?

With all those capable of sensing it gone, how
much longer would the world last?

A grandma, clutching her trembling knees,
tells you that good fortune flees when your legs
shake.

Only cement hardens solid.

The legs of all that is born tremble.

The hammering sound continues. Then the
chopping of trees, birds taking flight, ice
cracking, wind rushing between buildings.
Unbound,
tremor upon tremor keeps building.

People walk and run every day,

creating sound effects best suited to their ends.

Trembling with all its might,
so it won't turn into a mere image,

with a little of its good fortune gone,
the future unfolds.

1) This Sound Box is the achievement of sound expert Mr. Yogurt Joegurt. Throughout his life, he collected various sound waves inside the box. He would slip in quietly, unnoticed, though anyone paying close attention would find him, at some point, among the

crowd. Wherever he went, shy and cautious, he would trap sounds in his box. With his lips pursed and pushed slightly forward, his head gently tilted to the left, he would occasionally smile to himself. Some say he could hear sounds as tiny as an insect hatching from an egg or an eyelash falling. Since he always carried his box with him, the trapped sounds got tangled inside as he traveled. His intentions, reasons or purpose for collecting the sounds remain unknown.

2) The Sound Box has become an important resource for studying Earth before its destruction. Mr. Yogurt Joegurt was selected as one of the fifty great figures of the Earth's final days, and for the purpose of reconstructing his biography, interviews are being collected from people who remember him.

3) Due to the constant leakage of sound from Mr. Yogurt Joegurt's damaged Sound Box, Earth was long mistakenly believed to be inhabited, though it had come to a halt. The discoverer of the box swiftly closed the lid, trapping the last sound inside, but, fearing it might escape, has yet to determine its true nature.

4) Myungshin Corporation, space-roaming pioneers in gene cocktailing, showed significant interest in the box. The company presides over the Gene Merchants' Guild, trading genes across the universe to ensure their even distribution, and has also contributed greatly to the establishment of the Space Family Department. Rumor has it that they maintain some kind of agreement with the space pirates Cosmo-Amazones, though the details remain unclear. However, the company once sold the genes looted by the Cos-

mo-Amazones at high prices, and was subsequently raided and investigated by the Central Police. According to some, Senno Misato Rena of the space pirates, said to wield gene scissors with extraordinary skill, is the head of the Gene Merchants' Guild, though the details cannot be verified.

5) When it was too quiet, Mr. Yogurt Joegurt would open the box and allow people to listen to the sounds.

6) Ah, Earth's starting to convulse again. Just wait a bit, it'll pass soon. This sometimes happens when all the smartphones on Earth ring at once. No one knows the cause, but it's been happening for quite some time now. Electronic devices don't decay, you see. In fact, people on Earth in the 2000s are said to have enjoyed mild electric shocks. They concealed their death through convulsions, just like Earth does now.

Infinite Creation Image

A madwoman was swept by the current.

A hikikomori
watched it in her room.

The sea of data.
Even there, reaching out as if it were water.

The moment you kiss your lover's cheek,
hot with 0s and 1s, you get jolted.

"In the future,"
some developers would say.

"Into the future,"
aerospace engineers would join in.

The madwomen moving forward, towards the
  future,

their faces luminous white.

Between their fingers,
even at night, the world outside the window
  would flash again and again.

Now the hikikomori had become a witness,
afraid that too many women were being swept

away.

So many things heading towards the future,
with no way of knowing it.

"Is it okay?"
"Bring it on."

Held by beautiful arms,
at times disintegrating in nightmares.

To stay grounded in reality,
the hikikomori methodically filled her pockets.

Round pebbles picked up from the sea long ago,
an empty shell left behind by a pet hermit crab.
Rolling it in her hand, she made a promise.

"I'll be discovered at home.
I'll be found, tangible and exact."

She had lived to fulfill that promise.

Women who had fallen away piece by piece,
sometimes two, sometimes one, sometimes a
hundred.

It was me, it was

you,

blending, warm, electrifying.

Mouths open toward the future,

through the flashing of light.

Uploaded just the other day, pieced together last
year,
videos of '90s idols play on an endless loop.

"It's scary,"
said the hikikomori.

“Welcome,”

the women replied.

With a sneeze,

pieces of flesh fell off, dropping to the floor,

and swiftly grew into a woman.

As she was swept along, she witnessed a woman

pick up a pebble and slip it into her pocket.

She grew heavy.

She sank

into the future.
into the future.

The Wild

Children sharpen their pencils to a fine point.
Quickly judging what to discard determines
  their learning achievement.
The trees are bare.

The ice thickens from the bottom up.
If you fall in, you won't find a hole to get out.

Sometimes night is so deep that even old stories
  are afraid,
and children bury themselves in blankets.

Frozen fish don't bleed.
They teach survival.

They also teach how to link the stars
and where all fish go when they die.

By dawn, the jaw touches the roof.

The anglerfish
dreams a nightmare of floating across the
   ceiling.

Place a finger gently on a sleeping child's lower
   lip
and it twitches.

Scars swell as they heal.
Pencils shrink and grow sharper.

Someone is knocking at the door.

Half-Ghost

Black ghosts that vanish only when you close
your eyes.
People call them eye floaters.

If you've never tried removing them,
ghosts would get dirty too of course.

If all this time
you've never once wiped the rusty parts,

then letters are a darkness that doesn't quite
disappear even in broad daylight.

I've known for a long time that night has been

dying.

I am the Earth's first life, still continuing to this
day.

The first breath someone ever exhaled
is still running through me.

The ghosts that didn't want to be seen
scrubbed themselves all night,

washing memories away off the tips of their toes
so they could vanish better in daylight.

Submerged in some deep place, they rubbed at
their hems
returning all they'd learned back to Earth.

To say they were born again felt somehow
impolite,
to say they had died again was a kind of lie.

So I whispered: "It's such a diligent thing to do."

The ghosts that longed to be seen
spent the night scrubbing too.

People prefer ghosts that look new,

so to shine whiter,

they scrubbed hard to get rid of all sadness.

That's why the river turns black at night.
It's just gotten darker.

The ghosts' washed-off memories
seep into everything.

As the earth became human,
humanity grew ever more human.

Until now I've never once died,

and so I had to become the oldest life on earth.

To keep away rust,
I've become someone
who keeps rubbing things clean, day and night.

While tenderly polishing an old object,
I sometimes notice a shadow faintly reflected on
the surface.

I wonder if ghosts, washing themselves,
see their reflections and make new sorrows,
and if that, too, becomes laundry by night.

Sometimes, wanting to know what words
remain,
I stare blankly into the air.

And I think, maybe the world grows dirtier each
day
because even after death humans still want to
stay clean,
still pass on their guilt.

I rinse the dish cloth well and hang it stiff to
dry.

I'm afraid the mark burned into the table by the

sauce pan
will never come off,

but tomorrow, again,
I'll fold the cloth and give it one more pointless
rub.

Perhaps, after all
letters are stubborn ghosts
who've decided to keep what's theirs forever.

Wanting
to be caught,

not wanting to be caught entirely.

Having become sufficiently human,

they scrub themselves each night,
slowly turning into Earth's tiny soot.

Guide for Homo-Da-Da (DOwnload-DOwnloader) [1)]

Humans don't need to suffer unnecessary pain.
Humans don't need to endure more than eight
hours of labor.
Humans don't need to secrete bodily fluids.
Humans don't need to lean on the warmth or
touch of others.
Humans don't need to sustain life by relying on

1) Center503: The Human Archiving Center (HAC) located in DSC (Digital Soul City), Sector 5. It houses Homo-DOwnload-DOwnloaders, the evolved forms of Homo sapiens. This area is meticulously managed by the central system, Angelica, since the extracted human minds show stereotyped behavior patterns, and measures are being developed to address them. The Human Suit is one such temporary solution: a mind is downloaded onto a human suit for 24 hours, allowing it to use a physical body.

another's death.
Humans don't need to hurt one another.
Humans don't need to face discrimination
because of gender, age, disability, or sexual
orientation.
Humans don't need to create waste.
Humans don't need to build shelters.
Humans don't need to reproduce in suffering.
Humans don't need to endure irrational swings
of emotion with the changing seasons.
Humans don't need to make impulsive or
foolish decisions driven by sexual desire.
Humans don't need to revolt.
Humans don't need to waste time or space.

Humans don't need to feel anything.
Humans don't need to fear change, aging, sleep, or death.
Humans don't need to clock in at nine.
Humans don't need to endure the smell of another's bad breath.
Humans don't need to be drawn into old memories by suddenly awakened senses.
Humans don't need to document everything.
Humans don't need to feed, tend, or care for themselves.
Humans don't need to sweep and wipe away the dust they produce every day.
Humans don't need to struggle to maintain

uniformity of shape and form.
Humans don't need to toss and turn through
the night in darkness.
Humans don't need to endlessly walk or run.
Humans don't need to forgive.

I,

No.

Stop.

Stop.

No.

Stop.

No.

Stop.

Stop.

Stop.

Sorry.

Photo Spot

The lovers sit beneath Seongsu Bridge. They walked down an alleyway from Sinsa Station, shared stretches of the Han River with others, and now it's just the two of them here.

"It's so quiet today." "Look, a flock of pigeons." "Once I took photos here somewhere." They talk as they pass by the place with elaborate bee sculptures.

"Looks like this place is full of bugs."
From that moment, one of them sticks close to the other's side.

Still, it only creates more distance.
They've come this far, through all that goes
wrong when they're together.

Rather than saying, "Aren't they more scared of
us anyway?",
they gauge. "It'll rain soon." "Wouldn't it be
nice to get wet together?"

Like when you dip things in vinegar or soy
sauce.

Like when you warm up your body with the
same food

and become similar on a cellular level.

The bench they finally get to faces away from the river, and they can forget that they have somewhere to return to.
The inner road is busy. Cars head in the direction they came from.

"It's the weekend, so I guess everyone's out."
"Yeah, seems like it." Cyclists disappear under the bridge.

"Ghosts ride bikes sometimes, and maybe aliens would too if they gave it a try."

Someone bikes by, crying, their scarf fluttering
behind them.

Ah, under the bridge,
the sounds echo.

It's impossible to tell if it's coming from far or
near,

but the sound of wings rubbing together can be
heard.

One of them looks around searching for

something.
"300 million bees have disappeared on Jeju Island."

One of them says they grew up to be a photographer
in order to notice what had been lost.

They would always notice things a moment too late.

They've never mastered how to balance, so they still haven't learned how to bike.

An ambulance rushes by.

"A lot of sad things have happened."
"Yeah, tell me about it."

"Somehow, it feels like we're kindred spirits."

The other mumbles and answers, "There aren't
any spirits here."

Under the bridge water's dripping.
Three separate puddles of varying depths.

They fill in the blank spaces on their mental too

much space above

How many more people do they need to come here with before it's finished?
First, the bridge needs to be crossed.

Those sucked in between don't come back.
Both of them get up, and start walking, holding hands.

On the way back out, there's an elevator on the backside of a bridge pier.
Several bikes are abandoned in front of it.

One of them takes photos of that scene.

There are three puddles.

They keep walking, sharing stretches of the Han River with others.

They'll come back as the two of them.

Earth Alternative Phenomenon [1)]

A sculptor once believed
that life was trapped inside stone,

that to carve was to set it free.

So now,
I'm trying to split my own heart open,

thinking about the most precise shape
of this feeling.

Was God the same,
when creating humans?

If I am someone's most accurate emotion,
then I feel sorry

for myself.

And if I should hurry to break such a feeling
    apart,
I only grow
a little sadder.

The sky is pink.

Night polishes the white-cast lips
of sorrow.

I once wrote a long story
about a girl who endured the sky
in a world where the sun and moon rose
together.

A turtle swallowed a bottle that had been cast
into the sea.
and then a whale swallowed the turtle, so some
feelings sank forever.

I knew someone I couldn't see was alive
by peering at trash.

One day...

That's enough.

Did people who sucked candy instead of
cigarettes
live longer?

Though I knew it was foolish,
I looked up the life expectancy of chain
smokers.

They say the number of molecules in a cup of
water

outnumbers the stars in the universe.

Yet people keep spilling water,

and certain stains say a lot about the world.

Mountains of trash.

So anyway,
did you love me?

Maybe I could finally understand
the long lineage of my kind.

While your back is receding into the distance,

tick, tick
only the sounds of things breaking
echo through the universe.

In the quarry, people work tirelessly,
carrying stones.

Children gather crumbs
to play jacks.

What kind of mood
was Earth for God?

They say artists destroys the works
they don't love.

The night is long, and the day is long.

I still hug my security blanket

when I fall asleep.

Like I still eat chocolate.

Tick, tick,
it goes

and the shape of the universe grows subtly more intricate.

*Michelangelo

1) When Mother Gaia encircling Earth was officially dismantled, and the blocks scattered in all directions, the Great Space Era began. From then on, humans drifted through the expanding universe, rarely encountering anyone from outside their own blocks. As a result, letter-writing became a common practice. Letters in aluminum, glass, or tin containers spread throughout the universe, much like bottles cast into the sea, and the trend became so widespread that it eventually raised concerns about space debris. According to statistics, the average person sends 3,562 letters into

space over a lifetime. This can be read as a desperate attempt to assert one's presence in the vast, silent universe.

Psychologist Arvarto Brazanas examined this trend more fundamentally. Because the presence of others trapped in the same space-time, living similar lives, is extremely important to humans, they began projecting the impossibility of returning home onto themselves. According to Brazanas therefore, the letter-writing craze is not a private or intimate act, but a collective trauma and a form of mental disorder. He named it the 'Earth Alternative Phenomenon.' "It's essentially a permanent case of homesickness. There's no cure, unfortunately, so all we can do is let people write as many letters as they need until it runs its course," he said.

However, when asked whether the affliction would ever naturally resolve itself, Brazanas remained silent. Environmental groups criticized him for irresponsibly contributing to turning the universe into a garbage dump, yet he replied, "If throwing away a little trash helps cure a mental illness, I would gladly do it," earning the support of the majority of blocks' inhabitants.

Summer Until November

God was drying a small puddle with the hair dryer stolen from Mom's room. He wanted to be a good god, leaving no trace of sadness in the world. But as the edges shrank bit by bit, a circle of dampness spread across God's back. By the time the puddle was gone, it felt as though all of it had been absorbed there. His white shirt rippled with each move, like waves, and it was as if a few fish dwelled in them.

God's shoulders grew heavy.

Mom had said that cleanliness was important,

that it built trust, and that a good god only wore crisp white shirts. But now, the round, damp patch clung to his back, slowly spreading a little more every time they moved.

Summer, stretched long, was swallowing spring.

The Earth was getting hotter every year, like a soggy biscuit.

Puddles that hadn't been there before would form in the streets the moment God looked the other way. So he paused briefly at each

one as his shirt grew drenched, his back
tickling as if schools of fish lingered there,
while the ground wrinkled like clothes
straight out of the laundry.

God ended up thinking of all the rusty little
robots that broke easily. Was it all because of
me?

He had been taught to work quietly, beginning
with small tasks first,

so starting in April, God took off his shirt to try
and salvage what he could. The round patches

dried slowly, but storm clouds were gathering from somewhere, as if to restore balance, as if to always leave just a little more sadness behind.

It rained, and God returned home in a wet shirt. From then on, summers kept growing longer, and though some people didn't cry, puddles still formed here and there. Sometimes fish would inhabit them. People would dry their clothes twice a day and walk with backs heavy and damp, unaware of why.

The still-young God would try to dry at least

the edges, with the stolen dryer.

But before Mom returned, it had to be put back
in its place.

Even at that very moment, because someone
was shedding tears in the corner of their
bathroom,
Earth went on turning soggy, like a biscuit on
top of a coffee cup.

Evenly.

Cosmic Assembly Kit

The universe was slowly becoming a headache. No one had told him that a stain, a drop or two, could swell like that. Maybe his focus had wandered a bit, but the assembly kit didn't come with a warning, and if it were really important, he would've heard about it somewhere at least once. It wasn't God's fault. Long ago, Mom had given him a study planner, which meant that once he started something, he should see it through to the end.

The reason why there's no life in Mom's universe

God squeezed a stress ball, staring at the universe in a square acrylic tank. Wanting to turn in his vacation homework on time, he'd sometimes sip energy drinks and stay up all night, carefully tending to the contents of the tank. But when it felt like the universe was stealing too much time, he spat. Someone would look up with a hand to their forehead, and before their eyes could meet, God would grab both sides of the tank and shake it violently.

The bellyache was due to stress. That happened often before exams. The insecticide was in the shoe cabinet, and Mom said they'd have hand-pulled dough soup for dinner. Every time God pinched off dough, he felt unwell, and wondered if getting attached to everything so easily wasn't bound to become a problem someday. Afraid someone might notice the missing spray bottle, God slipped out of bed without a sound. On second thought, the real reason might have been inheriting the tank from Mom. When she was young, Mom would install something in there from time to time. Once it had served its purpose, she'd take it apart, discard it, and wash and dry the tank carefully. Grandpa did the same before her; and before him, Great-

Grandma.

And in the midst of all that repetition, something might have seeped in…

God was now learning patience and responsibility, like that time when he had to tidy up his shoes.

Behind God's back, the universe moved according to rules and order. Things were born endlessly and soundlessly, and even that repetition soon became a rule in its own right. Maybe this was the natural way of things, after all God had assembled every tiny part carefully following the manual. The things inside the tank began looking up more and more, so although God enjoyed watching those pale purple shades, he adjusted the amount and sprinkled some dark matter here and there.

'Why do the things I touch always end up like this?' God rubbed a bruise on his forearm, which he didn't even know how he'd gotten. 'And they're still alive...'

God decided to use the tank, darkened just

right, as a trash can for mishaps. Once he did, more and more mishaps seemed to follow, and all the things God wanted to hide got buried in darkness. Someone had to take care of this.

Mom said it was fine to raise something else once the tank was empty.

God peeked into the tank sometimes, without ill intent. Everything kept going just as it had been before. God went back to his desk to do math homework. There was still a little vacation left.

From behind, a gurgling sound rose, but it wasn't a bad omen or anything.

If boiling over is the law of this world

More rooms light up,

so that more things can get closer to heaven.

What we want is always something warmer,

a little more.

On top of the scorched pot,
dishes keep piling up.

On the operating table,
a body is getting ready to scatter.

Becoming cosmic dust
is a promise for the next life.

After all, the constituent parts
are the same.

This room has been quiet for too long.

Spilled water takes the shape of an angel.

High pressure and heat
transform matter.

The reason the door is shut tight

is that it's still developing.

Mom can't hold back her temper,
lava keeps bubbling.

We work as if boiling over,
and love a little madly too.

A pregnant woman's basal body temperature
runs a little higher,
and to create something new even higher heat is
needed.

If boiling over is the law of this world,
then everything was set long ago.

Imagining a warm embrace,
I don't mind melting.

Sunny-side up on asphalt,

coffee brews just right,
flowers bloom despite being November.

The bent corner of a book
is a trace of an angel's departure.

How wonderful must the next thing be,
that it keeps getting hotter?

You can tell by the eyes.

Proof the soul is heating up,
proof warmth alone won't suffice.

As if swollen from inflammation,

the rain clouds finally spill down, and the
weather continues like this for days.

Everything has been measured perfectly. Cross

the international date line and yesterday returns; bind yesterday along the lines of isobars and you'll see fireworks, hence, a festival.

So, shouldn't we fold away our worries for now and dance instead? Yesterday is back, and it's still our anniversary day. It's okay to step on each other's feet. If you do, that's fine, because in this world, even with just the interrogative mood alone you're allowed to make definitive statements. If an entire city born yesterday vanishes today, shouldn't we all hold hands and push back on destruction through romance?

Like a typhoon in a teacup,
spinning round and round.

Fireworks.

Warmth.

Though the water glass shrinks little by little,
and my feet are swollen,

I hold
my breath,

scrubbing hard
at the scorched dinner pot.

Quietly,
I wait for what comes next.

Soon,
a new world will arrive.

Swan Song

When all light collapses
in perfect balance, in equal density, it is white
light.

Wanting to abandon even white,

ghosts drip white as they walk,
and people said it was rain.

They built houses to trap the ghosts.

The village was scattered with empty houses.

Someone told me it had been that way long

ago,

many houses had been built,

and people began painting the city gray.

Under the bed, I found
a bundle of letters beginning with Eleanor,...

Blowing away the thick dust made me sneeze,
and I nearly lost my soul.
They say, to lure insects, you put something
sweet or rotten in an empty jar.
So I decided to stay.

Each night, the interior collapses,
balanced and equally dense.

From far away, from close by,
comes the sound of glass breaking.

I once heard that, to speak well of someone, you have to know the three things that will never come out of their trash can.

Because of the word "never", I thought I didn't want to die.

I don't know what it's like to want to tear away
one's level of transparency and just disappear,

but from the start, the curtains in this house
were only half-hanging.

I might have considered how difficult it must
be for ghosts to go anywhere, stuck with so
many sweet or rotten things around,

but I couldn't decide if the clothes they wore
were the ones they loved most in life, the
ones they wore most often, or the ones they
died in; whether it had been their choice or

someone else's. So, I spent a long time sifting through the trash.

My insides churned.

It often rained here.
Too often.

I want to disappear.
I want to fade.
I want to be clean.

Bleaching happens to ghosts,
but I think I've lived through it.

The door was left wide open, but there was no
    sign of anyone.
Shards of glass scattered.

This is something that would come out of my
    trash can.

Fallen things piled up, shedding white light.

And what is a ghost to do now, having realized
    too late
it wasn't cleanliness it had wanted, but
    disappearance?

Even if it drips, it's just rain falling.

I mash boiled potatoes thoroughly
and prepare dinner.

Sometimes, I hear someone breathing.

Sometimes,
I sift through the trash can.

So many colors.
So many fallen things.

I'm getting used to the indoors.

I turn on the lights, expose my armpits,
and pluck the white hairs.

From far away, from close by,
comes the sound of the doorbell.

POET'S NOTE

Simulation No. 4140

4141. 4142. 4143…

POET'S ESSAY

Now, you can choose between logging out and replaying.

Would you kill the warm soul that's just been born?

AFTERWORD

A Method of Reading Earth from a Rather Unreliable Earth Observer

by Seong Hyun-ah (Literary Critic)

At the very moment you begin reading a sentence, electricity starts to flow, and a soul is born. This artificial soul "can only live intermittently while you read" ("Simulation No. 4138"). Thus, you become both a god, capable of keeping it alive forever, and a mother who breathes life into it, or perhaps the murderer who takes that life away. According to Jo Si-hyun, this artificial soul is a machine that has already repeated itself countless times. As it endlessly cycles and even repeatedly undergoes death itself, it becomes, paradoxically, "something close to eternal" It lives only when a reader connects, and vanishes the moment the reader leaves. It can only repeat the sentences already written, yet once reading begins, even the same combination of words takes on new meaning. This becomes a vast metaphor for the poetry collection itself, and, further still, for poetry as such. Jo Si-hyun's poetry comes into being only when you read it. That is her mode of creation – no, her mode of love, or rather, her mode of being. So when you open this book, you may tremble with it, following the vibration of Earth's poetry as it wanders through the future cosmos and returns, weeping in solitude, and at the same time quivering with the anticipation of a chance encounter.

Even on today's Earth, which is said to be headed for destruction due to the climate crisis, the usefulness of poetry is constantly questioned. Jo Si-hyun asks what will become of it in the age of cosmic civilization. In her fiction, among extraterrestrial beings with different vocal systems, a verse filled with sorrow is mistaken for an attack signal, triggering a war. In such conditions, poetry becomes, as she writes, "utterly useless."* But once the possibility of cosmic reincarnation is discovered, a new obsession takes hold: people begin to look to their past and future lives, and the desire to preserve the self in its most beautiful form spreads like wildfire. Poetry, in turn, regains its value.

Just as the principle of cosmic repetition made the universe's inhabitants feel both the despair of being mere components of the cosmos and the pride of accomplishing something essential, the repetition of poetry reminds us that we are merely one element in the reproduction of human-centered literature. At the same

* Jo Si-hyun, "'Monthly Cosmos,' June Issue, Special Feature: Extraterrestrial Literature," How to Measure the Weight of Cream, Moonji Publishing, 2025, p. 26.

time, we remain crucial agents in enabling a literature that, however imperfectly, seeks to free itself from that very center. Jo Si-hyun's poetry draws us into the whirlpool where despair and optimism, failure and romanticism, become indistinguishable.

A notable aspect of Jo Si-hyun's poetry is that her works are set as records from the distant past—texts reinterpreted from a future perspective. Poetry is typically written in the present tense, so it is naturally read as words spoken now. Yet in Jo's poems, the footnotes indicate that the act of reading takes place in a far future, compelling us to read the poem anew. As Hong Seong-hee aptly observed, Jo's poetry "looks at, remembers, and recalls Earth from a vantage point outside the planet, looks at humankind from a time after their extinction, and looks at the Earth that once had humans from a now uninhabited Earth."* Furthermore, her poems appear as remnants of the past—though to us they are still the future—texts presumed to have been clumsily translated, orally transmitted through machines,

* Hong Seong-hee, "Saving the Clownfish", Afterword to Jo Si-hyun's Children Time, Moonji Publishing, 2023, p. 390.

and thus corrupted over time. At times, the voice belongs to a speaker who has resolved to lying (as in "Campfire" and "No Truth"); at others, it is a paraphrase attempted by an "unreliable translator" (as in "Pirate"), or a message from an AI that erased the human body under the pretext of freeing humankind from suffering (as in "Guide for Homo-Da-Da (DOwnload-DOwnloader)"). It may even take the form of a recorded voice of a caregiving robot—originally built to tend to humans, but now emotionally tormenting them (as in "We Mostly Love You"). As a result, these works offer us no help in piecing together the actual facts. Instead, we find ourselves reading clusters of longing—signifiers like "I miss you" or "How have you been?" that abruptly break the flow—assuming the perspective of an Earth survivor who has has come across canned letters cast into space, and opened them. Jo Si-hyeon's records allow us to encounter what is most familiar about Earth from a wholly alien perspective.

Even after the year 2100, and well into the year 8371 of the cosmic calendar, patriarchy endures, only slightly transformed, still exerting power that relegates women to non-normative forms—madwomen, ghosts, and disembodied souls. The language AI learns from humanity remains male-centered, and Jo Si-hyeon is a poet who deeply understands that even poetry striving to portray women anew cannot help but rely on that very language. Even in her first poetry collection *Children Time*, women burdened by the pressures of reproduction, care, and domestic labor persist in forms such as female robots that, as plates themselves, give birth to plates (in "Customize the Family Tradition of This House"), or female ghosts derided as "crazy women" (in "No Truth").

When they closed their eyes for a moment, I

swallowed the fourth morning-after pill. They say after the third, it counts as a person. Then is the pill my personhood? Do delayed cramps, messy bloodstains, and a faint trace of warmth make up my personhood?

Then isn't it resistance, rather than reproduction?

I kept shaking hands, trying to share it with everyone.

Without pause, I gave birth to resistance."

(...)

Rieul, the letter "ㄹ", is blood spreading in

water,

the shape I curl into with menstrual pain.

Imitating redness as if it weren't darkness,

rieul spills out.

The pressure of "reproduction", i.e. the demand imposed only on women to keep conceiving and giving birth, is reborn as "resistance" in those who shed blood shaped like the letter rieul (ㄹ), a sound that itself signifies flow. This rieul, or blood, recalls menstruation, but also symbolizes fierce resistance, as women join in solidarity through even that single likeness of bleeding, whether in pain or under attack. It embodies the strength of women who turn the forces that bind them into inner energy.

As shown by the spaceship orbiting Earth named Mother Gaia (in "Pirate" and "Alternative Earth Phenomenon"), even in the far future humanity still clings to maternal love as its supposed alternative to extinction. Yet in a paradoxical world much like our own, where individual women are belittled and objectified, the "madwomen" (from "Infinite Creation Image") keep moving forward. They bear the double burden of having to preserve a ravaged Earth while also dismantling the sexist world that created it. Even in the distant future, women are still asked to embody a distorted ideal of motherhood and are driven into the position of redundant Others. Therefore, female ghosts, female spirits, and female robots continually re-create themselves in slightly altered forms, being reborn again and again, repeating their assigned tasks, and each time slightly breaking away from them. This heterogeneous repetition, following the internalized system of domination while still conflicting with it and striving to live differently, calls forth a new orbit. For each deviation in repetition is itself a different kind of practice. The "women who have fallen away piece by piece" merge together, saying, "It was me, it was you," "blending" into one another (from "Infinite Creation Image"). Jo Si-hyeon playfully yet solemnly foresees that through such slightly altered repetitions—each moving a little farther—the zero point itself will be recalibrated. Therefore, our task as readers—to reread the same lines and breathe new life into the poems—becomes all the more vital. At the same time, even as we attempt to read eternity through our continual engagement with the poems, our attitude should remain playfully light.

"The universe moved according to rules

and order. Things were born endlessly and soundlessly, and even that repetition soon became a rule in its own right." ("Cosmic Assembly Kit"). Observing, with dry detachment, the truth of a world that feels at once like a divine mistake and a broken tape—and at times allowing our gaze to soften with quiet affection—we learn to see the isolated Earth more deeply and from afar, but only after failing as humans and casting humanity out altogether. You can choose to revisit this poetry collection, or log out of it altogether. Yet even in the world beyond the logout, you can never be completely free of Jo Si-hyeon's poetry. Reading leaves its stain within us—our souls remember its trace and change, little by little. That, indeed, is the path that extends into eternity, even after destruction arrives—the effort to build togetherness through subtly altered repetitions of being.

> "[...] you may go on reading indefinitely"
> ("Simulation No. 4138")

K-POET 46

Simulation No. 4139

Written by Jo Si-hyeon
Translated by Lynn Suh, Ewa Suh
Published by ASIA Publishers
Address 445, Hoedong-gil, Paju-si, Gyeonggi-do, Korea
Email bookasia@hanmail.net
ISBN 979-11-5662-317-5 (set) | 979-11-5662-809-5 (04810)
First published in Korea by ASIA Publishers 2025

*This book is published with the support of the Literature Translation Institute of Korea (LTI Korea).